THE GOBLIN'S RULES OF THE GAME

A GUIDE FOR LIVING LIFE

SEAN ÄABERG

P.O. Box 90296
Portland, OR 97290 USA
www.goblinko.com

The Rules were first written in June of 2018 for my "The Goblin" column in PORK magazine. We turned The Rules into a poster soon after. I wrote them quickly, off the cuff, with only grammatical edits from Katie & as a way to fill magazine space. Every year or so, I'd have the overwhelming feeling about whether I would feel okay with the magazine if I was dead. This was the longest project I've continuously worked on in my life. Seven years & 29 issues. I wrote The Rules as a way of trying to tell people what I had learned over time & how I felt that success could be found on a very personal level. Not based on my criteria, but on your criteria. I didn't want it to feel preachy or judgmental, just matter of factual or even obvious. Centrally, I wanted it to be helpful.

ISBN: 9781648412394
Printed in Portland, Oregon

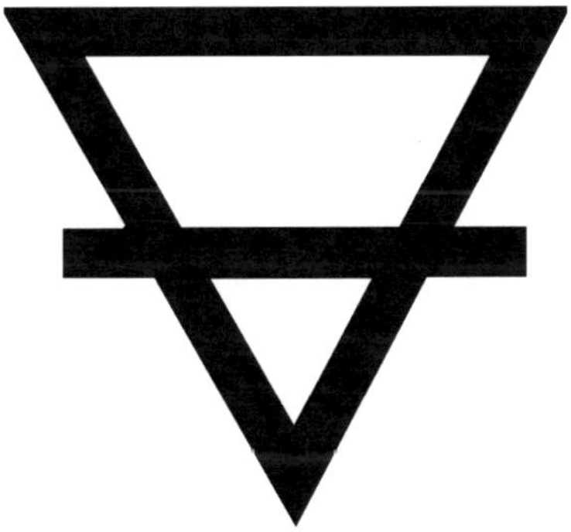

2018. I had just left for five days away from my family & work for the first time ever spending time with my ailing mother in late Winter, then she passed that Spring. The trip was bookended by a beautiful, cold, snowy passage through the mountains that separate Oregon from California. A thick blanket of snow laid over the land obscuring & darkening most details. Everything looked frosted, black & white. I was very close to my mother. We used to have long talks where I could actually feel my mind expand. Her death is a tremendous loss in my life. Her absence created a period of intense change & growth, I was meditating a lot on death. Dungeon Degenerates was exploding & we could afford to not just have our noses to the grindstone constantly.

It was the day after Katie's birthday, September 18th, or I guess it was the 19th because it was one in the morning. I found myself unable to breathe in the bathroom, Katie called emergency. When I awoke I found myself in the hospital, surrounded by loved ones. My brain was so oxygen starved that I thought I was in a Reality TV show for the next few weeks. People that came to see me were guest stars & I marveled at the attention to detail. Once I figured out that I had suffered a stroke, the first thing I thought was, "Things like this don't happen to me." But, it did happen to me. I had a major stroke, died, was resuscitated & spent the next three months in the hospital. The left, dominant side of my body was paralyzed, I couldn't speak, I had a tracheotomy (breathing hole in my neck), there was fluid being drained out of my skull through a tube, I was being fed with a tube in my stomach & that was just the major things. Most of my system was totally weakened & dependent on machines. Decades of burning the candle at both ends, periods of heavy drinking, constant caffeine abuse & not seeing a doctor will do that to you, or rather, me. I was strangely accepting of it all & recognized it as temporary either way. I knew the eerie calm of a deer in the jaws of a wolf.

Katie put The Rules up on the door of my room & doctors, nurses & guests would stop, read them, agree & then be shocked that the author was in the room with them, lying in the bed, hooked up to machines. It was cool to see something that I had written to pad out my column taking on a life of its own & be accepted with a universality that I hadn't seen before, for people like doctors & nurses & not the assorted varieties of Rockers I had been spending time with. I enjoyed seeing that I could reach out of my bubble, beyond my herd. Over time I've come to see my role as someone who leads people out of the herd, not as a part of any herd. Herd mentality pisses me off no matter the herd, always. So, this screed relies a lot on thinking for yourself, which is of prime importance to me.

Here is PORK 29, what would turn out to be the final issue. I feel like it is best to end things on an up beat, so this issue wasn't the planned end, although it ended up being the last issue produced before I had the stroke. The magazine would basically be undoable without the burning of the candle at both ends, working & playing too hard, doing the PNW distribution myself, from the trunk of our car hustler methodology (inspired by E40) that I had been operating under for a decade. Even though or because I have this DIY Punk ethos as my spine, I have always worked too hard. This hard work was going to build up my family, I was replicating the traditional American workhorse without realizing it. I saw myself more in the James Brown "Hardest Working Man In Showbiz" mode.

The Goblin's Rules for the Game

1. Life is a game. There are rules but there are only unofficial guidebooks written by the feeble minds of humans who do their damnedest to game the system. You can cheat & use a guidebook, but remember that it's unofficial & that nothing can overshadow experience & genuine skill. You will note that the guidebooks usually cost something.

2. You have to beat every level. There is no way to skip ahead, if you go too far ahead in the game all of the minor-enemies & mini-bosses will come after you & you won't know when they'll show up & in how many numbers! It's better to beat the level you're on thoroughly, even trying it a few times to get comfortable with your new abilities.

3. Talk to everyone. You never know when the guy who is standing mysteriously still by the rose bush will tell you about a new mission you have to go on. You never know when the Mexican Ninja will reveal the secret of lemons against witchcraft & the mystery of the chakras. Not all of the missions are worth pursuing, but you'll figure that out through trial & error.

4. If the game is too easy, you're not advancing. The processing of the human soul is difficult & the goal is to continue advancing through experience & to take on each challenge correctly in order to refine our spiritual energy. I'm serious! Don't look at me like that.

5. The easiest answers have the hardest questions & in their simplicity the complexity of existence is revealed. But you have to be able to ask the question. Write down the rules as you figure them out.

6. Avoidance stalls the game out. You can stop advancing in life & try to just stay in the same place, but the perpetual advancement of the universe will start throwing major obstacles & enemies in your way to get you out of that holding pattern. The universe would rather kill you then have you stall out if you're going to waste your life. Don't waste your quarter.

7. The human mind only interprets what it perceives as reality. We do not know what reality is - but we feel reality intuitively. All expressions of reality are interpretations. Follow your nose.

8. People will try to tell you what the game is but they are always wrong. They will create games inside of the game & tell you that they have the game. They don't. The game is different for every player. Games inside of the game are just games.

9. You are the final boss.

XOX SEAN ÄABERG, PORTLAND, OREGON

1. LIFE IS A GAME. THERE ARE RULES BUT THERE ARE ONLY UNOFFICIAL GUIDE BOOKS WRITTEN BY THE FEEBLE MINDS OF HUMANS WHO DO THEIR DAMNEDEST TO GAME THE SYSTEM. YOU CAN CHEAT & USE A GUIDEBOOK, BUT REMEMBER THAT IT'S UNOFFICIAL & THAT NOTHING CAN OVERSHADOW EXPERIENCE & GENUINE SKILL. YOU WILL NOTE THAT THE GUIDE BOOKS USUALLY COST SOMETHING.

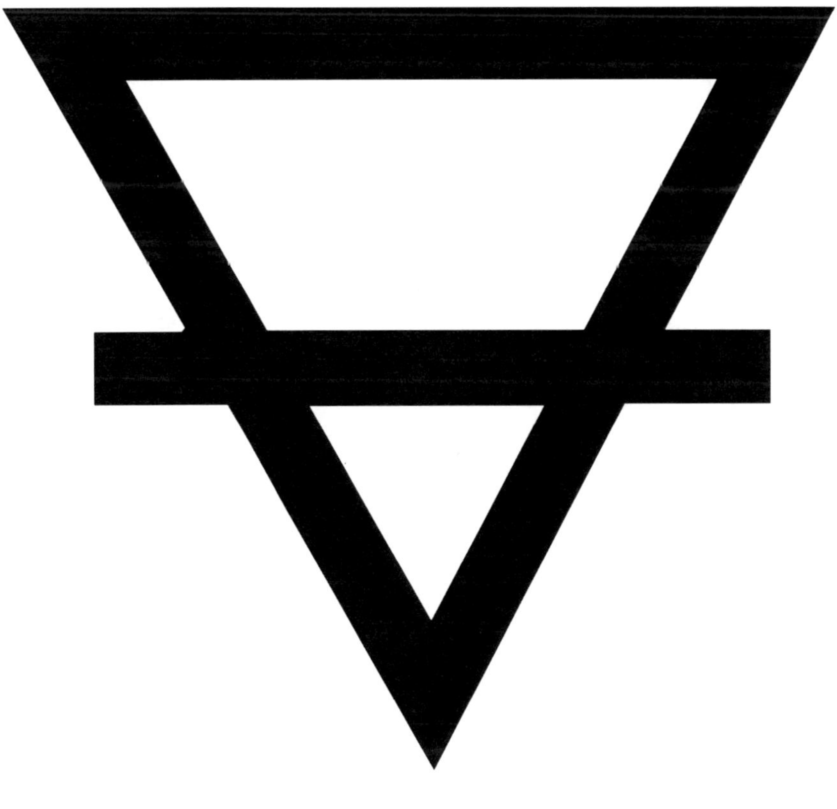

Games have been modeled after the structures that have been observed in life. Saying that life is a game isn't an attempt to simplify things, life is just as complicated as it is going to be. You don't really get a choice over that. My intention is to point out the structure or skeleton of life so that you understand what you're dealing with underneath all the complicated details. Our innate sense of this background order has informed how we think of & create games. Games are a reflection of this order.

I am not trying to create a game within life. I'm not trying to get you stuck in my rut. Even though my rut works very well for me, I also know that I have custom made it for me, not for you. I want you to think of this game like a well-tailored outfit, custom made to fit every contour of your body. Life is the most important, so this way of thinking is equally important. My goal is to point out that life unfolds like a game, this is my observation, not a belief. I have made these observations from my eyes to my brain. My eyes function normally, my eyesight is fantastic. My brain is a different story; I'm an artist & a Punk, I might be functionally crazy, I have brain damage from the stroke & I'm really smart. It's not a normal brain, but that's why I'm able to come up with cool ideas that aren't expected. I'm just trying to be above board & lay everything on the table. Life is a game that you must figure out the rules to, the characters, the themes, everything. Once you figure out that first bit, the rest is much more difficult. It's the actual living of life, there is no alternative. The game unfolds at its own pace. Another goal for me is to assure you that life has meaning & is not just a mess of chaos as so many believe. Again, this comes from observation, not from a belief I hold. I'm interested in the nature of reality, not the bolstering of people's beliefs. That said, there is a surface layer of chaos that hides the fact that the world is intensely ordered.

When I was a kid & going to school, it was obvious to me that I was stuck in someone else's trap, in someone else's game. The scene for the song "Education" in Pink Floyd's the Wall showing school children getting ground up into sausage was very impactful on me. I like sausages, including how they are made, but I have no interest in being ground up as sausages! Most kids were put in the same school game & the rules & outcomes are clearly defined in a way that puts parents at ease, provides steady employment for some & sucks up people's tax dollars. They even issue report cards to grade how you are doing in their game. It's a way of trying to control people who have their whole life ahead of them, a way of trying to control & direct society. I don't have a very charitable view of compulsory education; we chose to homeschool our kids because of this. I want my kids to have their own destiny to figure out, without starting it all out in someone else's game. Some people do very well in that trap, especially people who grew up in a situation worse than schooling, for them the relative safety of schooling is comforting. It's very difficult to argue with those kinds of creature comforts, so I won't.

People have tried to write official guide books to life since time immemorial. There is a new one every day! People have said "this is the only book" but that's obviously not true & you only have to look at the full shelves of libraries & bookstores to see the falsity of this. It is a field full of charlatans, lunatics, flakes & fools. I definitely have some of those aspects to myself. That is probably why I am drawn to writing a text such as this! I have no doubt about this & want you to know. Only you can tell if I am worth listening to. I am doing my best to be clear. People also try & get God to co-author their book, but there cannot be proof of this. Declaration of that kind of authority is always questionable, it reveals a lot about controlling & impatient tendencies of the author. "Look, my co-author is the boss!"

Undoubtedly there are books that are inspired, but ultimately they are written by the hands & minds of men, even if they are divinely inspired.

These guide books always cost something because the writing of them is an industry! This zine is no different, pointing out that a thing costs money is not dismissive, it's just an attempt at pointing out the obvious. Pointing out the obvious is necessary these days, it's a symptom of being able to communicate with most everyone & not having common assumptive footing. These books aren't handed out at birth, they are written by people who developed a system for looking at life for people looking for a set of rules. Even if these books were handed out at birth, they would just be handed out by people who say that they have some kind of unprovable authority.

2. YOU HAVE TO BEAT EVERY LEVEL. THERE IS NO WAY TO SKIP AHEAD, IF YOU GO TOO FAR AHEAD IN THE GAME ALL OF THE MINOR-ENEMIES & MINI-BOSSES WILL COME AFTER YOU & YOU WON'T KNOW WHEN THEY'LL SHOW UP & IN HOW MANY NUMBERS! IT'S BETTER TO BEAT THE LEVEL YOU'RE ON THOROUGHLY, EVEN TRYING IT A FEW TIMES TO GET COMFORTABLE WITH YOUR NEW ABILITIES.

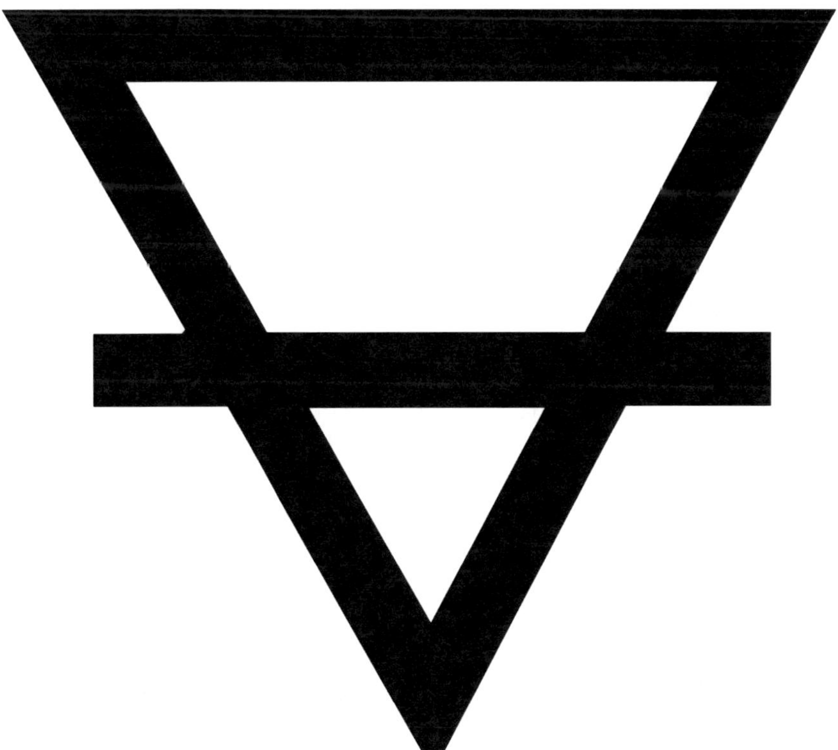

With hindsight you can see that different phases of life were levels in that they have a clear character, difficulty, theme & even a particular aesthetic or theme song. Sometimes it's clear that a level is made up out of a bunch of smaller levels. There are heroes & villains that make themselves plain, only to vanish in the mists of time. Sometimes the characters in the game are with you for a long time, sometimes even your whole life! It is especially easy to see if you have written the events of your life down. If you feel that these events aren't worth writing about, that is an indicator that you aren't doing enough with your life or some kind of insecurity.

Life unfolds at its own pace, there is no way to skip ahead. Growing up takes an entire childhood & yet, people try to skip that part & go straight to adulthood. Scratch the surface of many of these adults & they are still a screaming, pouty, misbehaving child on the inside. I can remember being a kid & intensely looking forward to the years when I would finally be an adult & out of school & free. I still had to live life in those years & grow & change & seek new things & not be one of those dreaded children who peak in their early life. There's a lot of years after the eighth, twelfth or fifteenth to live! I realize that the abstract idea of freedom was more of what I was interested in, not skipping ahead. Similarly, when I was young, I recognized I would do well as an old man (if I made it that far). This wasn't so much as wanting to skip ahead, but more aligned with where I'm at psychologically.

That said, you have to thoroughly clear each level or else the level comes after you & tries to force you to complete it. It's almost like a living, vengeful entity. The characters will pursue you to make sure your business is dealt with. If you lose out on completing a task, it can weigh on you heavily. You can try to skip a level, but if you want to advance in life, you must clear each level, they have been set up in front of you & the Universe acts like it's an insult to ignore the work. People feel lost because they have misplaced what they are supposed to have been doing all along, playing someone else's game. There can be a lot of resentment from these people living other people's games.

Once a level is cleared it's obvious, things empty out & there is a sense of repetition. At this point you might feel the need to fight the final boss. Most times you aren't ready for this fight, having been untested in life's other challenges. Some people die at this point, usually through some fault of their own. The real goal is to figure out what's going on with the next level. There will be clues, but centrally you will feel a pull. A lot of people feel so comfortable in the level where they are that they don't want to move on. Sometimes that pull can be some level you already cleared or unfinished business haunting you.

3. TALK TO EVERYONE. YOU NEVER KNOW WHEN THE GUY WHO IS STANDING MYSTERIOUSLY STILL BY THE ROSE BUSH WILL TELL YOU ABOUT A NEW MISSION YOU HAVE TO GO ON. YOU NEVER KNOW WHEN THE MEXICAN NINJA WILL REVEAL THE SECRET OF LEMONS AGAINST WITCHCRAFT & THE MYSTERY OF THE CHAKRAS. NOT ALL OF THE MISSIONS ARE WORTH PURSUING, BUT YOU'LL FIGURE THAT OUT THROUGH TRIAL & ERROR.

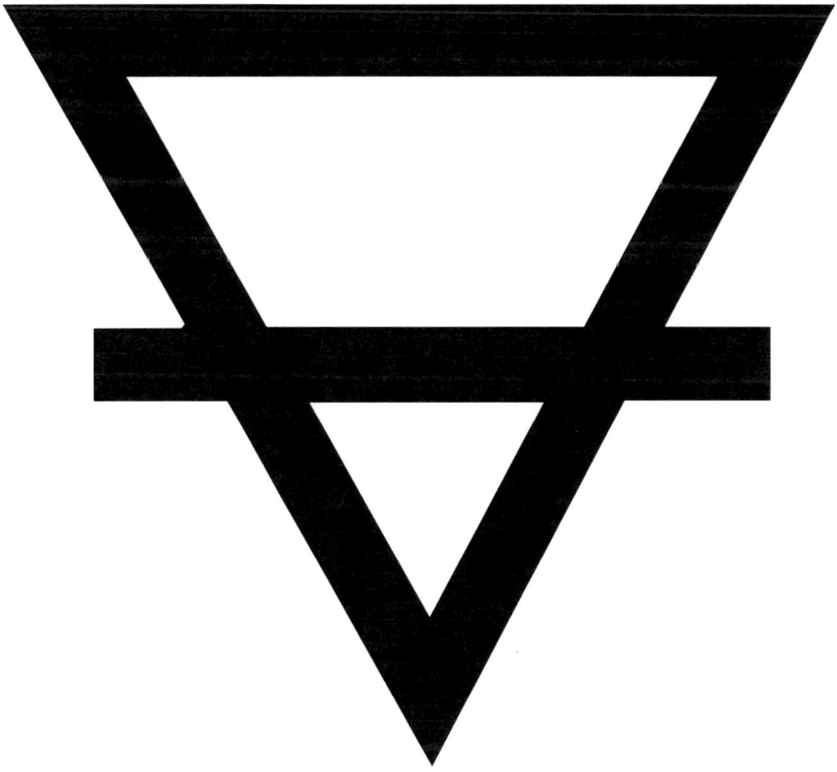

You can't know who you are going to meet & what sorts of things they might open up for you. Everyone is playing the game & has some sort of hints to give you. Are the hints good or bad? Unfortunately the only way to find out is living life. This doesn't mean you should go into these interactions unguarded, or go on all the missions, be smart, but also be open to all the experiences of people who are trying to figure out the game too.

When I started feeling trapped by life, I turned things that people told me into missions. I have a mission from Eugene of making Chicken Cordon Bleu given to me by the lady that worked at the surplus bread store that has been hanging over my head for over fifteen years! My wife doesn't like Bleu Cheese OR ham & doesn't eat pork! Anyhow, it's easy, just listen & you'll note the mission being set out in front of you. Some people are so unsure of themselves, they are unable to see levels, characters & missions that are right in front of them. Sometimes you need someone else who can see things clearly to see them for you. Think of them as an interpreter, but remember that you're getting second hand information that is being filtered through the complexities of a human mind.

There are some people you want to meet, but there are others you are destined to meet. People you didn't even realize existed, but have something to learn, something to share. These people might seem unimportant but you never know. Some people are total wastes of time & others will set you back, but the thing is, it's difficult if not impossible to know these things about people when you meet them or just before meeting them unless you have terrific abilities. People change, who you are & other people change, life is a constantly moving target. Different people interact with other people differently, sometimes a negative for one can be positive for another. So again, you're only going to figure this out through experience & other people are going to give you their views or collective folk wisdom.

the Mexican Ninja

In the summer of 1995 I was day drinking on the streets of Berkeley with my band "the Masked Men". It was warm, sunny & the sun shone on the concrete intensely. It was the Chaos Days USA, an event I put out the call for after reading about the Chaos Days the year previous in Hanover, Germany. The idea was to bring all the Punks to the streets of Berkeley for three days of... whatever would happen when you get that many Punks together for only the reason of being Punk. We were hanging out on Telegraph as we did & were going to our friend Fritz's game store the Art of War to drink before going to a show at 924 Gilman Street. On the way we ran into this short, Mexican street guy, he was probably around 40, sunburnt & drunk. I note that he was Mexican because he could barely speak English & it seemed like he had only been in the US for a few weeks. These are the kinds of people I would hang out with on the streets all the time. This man revealed that he used to be a police officer in Mexico. After drinking a bunch of my Country Club malt liquor (my chosen brand, I liked the mix of it obviously being a ghetto drink, aspiring to Country Club status), he showed us the "chakras" pin he wore for good luck on the inside of his blue gas station jacket. It was a swastika pin, which everyone was a combination of spooked, amused & confused by. Those combinations of feelings made me uncomfortable, I felt like a child around this symbol. I could tell that I needed to grow up. A mission opened itself up to me. As he offered to "share tobacco" & took us to the hiding place where he kept his papers in a Mason jar, we passed a lemon tree. He took a lemon & pronounced its powers "against witchcraft". Noted. Eventually after a couple of weird, rambling hours we escaped his gravity & headed to the Art of War in Oakland. None of us had cars so we walked a lot & sometimes took the bus. At this point in life I had been out of school for a year & the number of missions, levels & characters making themselves known to me was almost overwhelming. There were a lot of directions to go & things to do.

Chaos Days

Germany, the 80s. After several Punk meetings in Wuppertal, considered forerunners of Chaos Days, the first Chaos Days occurred in Hanover. The gathering was intended to protest a police plan to create a reference library of photographs of German Punks. Thereafter, Chaos Days were held starting in 1983.

I really liked the idea of large numbers of Punks just being around, disrupting things with their existence. It's a glorious idea, especially with the fashion of Chaos Punks. So much spikey, colorful hair, spiked & studded & painted leathers & bondage pants. Reminder that this was the 90s & the rot we're currently experiencing was no way as profound as it is now.

The most well-known Chaos Days took place in August 1994 (which I read about in the Oakland Tribune), 1995 & 1996. In 1995 I put out the call for a Chaos Days USA to be held in Berkeley, CA. Meanwhile in Germany in 1995 2,000 Punks & squatters fought with police, resulting in over 100 injured police officers & 450 arrested young people. The program had listed: "Friday 3 pm: Street fights. Saturday 11 am: Games with fire. Sunday: Glass-breaking demonstration." The result was riots & the destruction of cars & buildings. Two supermarkets were looted. These Chaos Days were the main topic of TV debates & newspapers for several weeks.

4. IF THE GAME IS TOO EASY, YOU'RE NOT ADVANCING. THE PROCESSING OF THE HUMAN SOUL IS DIFFICULT & THE GOAL IS TO CONTINUE ADVANCING THROUGH EXPERIENCE & TO TAKE ON EACH CHALLENGE CORRECTLY IN ORDER TO REFINE OUR SPIRITUAL ENERGY.

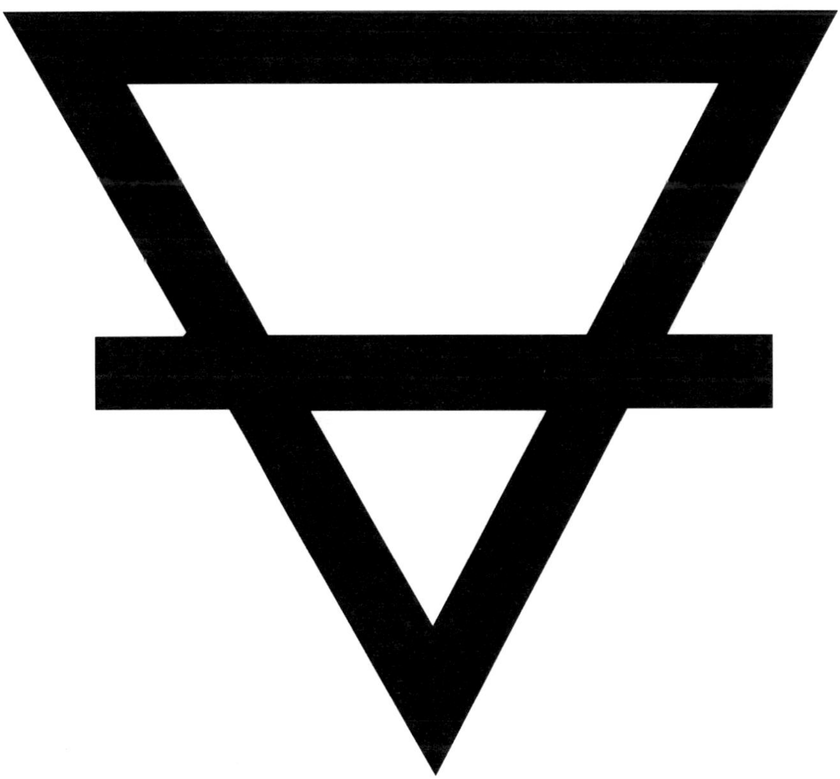

Life is hard. There isn't really any way around it. You can try & live an easy life, many do, but sometimes that can stagnate more than an individual, sometimes it can be a whole family, city or even a country. There are plenty of people & it is the trend to think you are good enough where you are at. There is some truth to this, you are good enough now, but there is always room to improve. Whatever your inadequacy it shouldn't be held against you. "Good Enough" or "Already Good" is a mentality of people who are stuck, frequently intergenerationally. A lot of the world's problems come from the pursuit of ease. Unattended to missions, characters & levels pile up around the place & start to disintegrate. Even if these things are just picked up on as energy, they complicate things & even rot like unused food in a refrigerator. Think of this game energy like water, it is best to keep it moving. Things rot, decompose & drown in it if it isn't allowed to flow. Maybe rot isn't the best word.

Sometimes life can be too hard, to the point where it feels punishing. Sometimes life is so easy, it's boring. Life should always be hard, but not too hard. The goal should be a manageable balance. If there is too much surplus of either, that is the mission at hand. Clear the boredom, clear the difficulty. Your brain, as with depression, is tainted by these things & will tell you that there is no other option but the status quo. The thing is, change is the only constant, the status quo is a hopeful creation of people's brains but it doesn't really exist outside of that, especially these days.

The refinement of spiritual energy can so easily be dismissed as New Age mumbo jumbo that I am amazed it came out of my mouth. So, like I said earlier on, these are observations I've made that aren't based on some sort of belief system, I'm a Happy Nihilist. So, while they are definitely skewed by my brain they aren't additionally skewed by some belief system. But, I am only human, so I undoubtedly have some prejudices, things I was raised around. For instance, I am interested in the abstract concept of success. I recognize this is a personal value & people that romanticize failure (frequently on the backs of generational success) think you're an asshole for daring to be successful. The thing those people are not seeing is that like everything else, true success is self defined. So again, this is less about belief than observation. The energy that goes into animating our body is the spirit & this energy can be refined over time, by following what the game is telling you to do. This same energy can be debased by not properly playing the game & it can really be rotted out with drugs & alcohol that prevent life from being lived.

5. THE EASIEST ANSWERS HAVE THE HARDEST QUESTIONS & IN THEIR SIMPLICITY THE COMPLEXITY OF EXISTENCE IS REVEALED. BUT YOU HAVE TO BE ABLE TO ASK THE QUESTION. WRITE DOWN THE RULES AS YOU FIGURE THEM OUT.

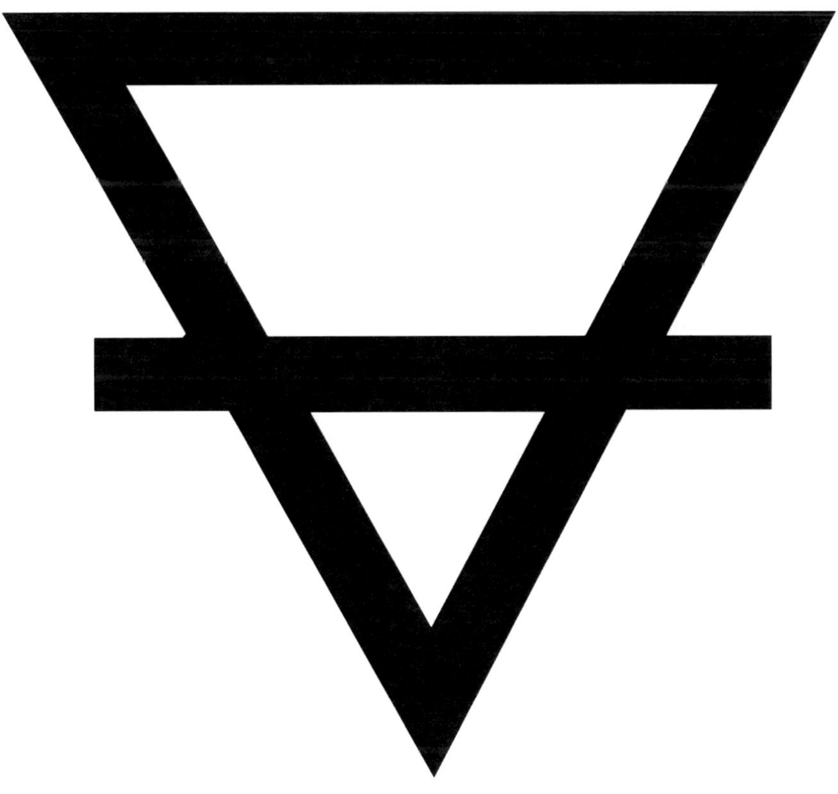

This is difficult & contradictory, people want things to be more complicated & too simple all at once. In reality, things are just the opposite. It's like the central tenet of this screed, life is a game. It's simple to understand but to find out the rules, missions, levels, characters etc is very difficult & then you must actually do the thing, this is the true challenge. Initially simple, in the end as complicated & messy as life, there is no escaping it. A minute to learn, a lifetime to master! The initial entry into the game is easy, it only requires a little bit of understanding, but once you're engaged it's almost endlessly complicated.

What is the question that you have to ask? It's "Why is life a game?" This question contains the notion that life is indeed a game, which is almost enough. This question also establishes that the Universe has some kind of order to it. Even though it is superficially chaotic there is an order to everything that comes into focus the more you look. Life can seem chaotic to people who haven't been keeping up with their game. This is another trick of the game, if you haven't been playing it's difficult to see.

Engaging your mind is also difficult, that's why I suggest writing things down. Writing down words transmits them into your memory in a different way than just reading them. Since having the stroke it has been more difficult to write things down, even to type. So, I repeat things I want to remember a few times in my head & it works similarly, I don't forget things that I need to remember. My brain goes at a much more manageable pace since the stroke, it could be the brain damage, who knows? I also haven't had caffeine in any substantial amount since then. I'm sure my uncaffeinated brain adds to the calming effect.

6. AVOIDANCE STALLS THE GAME OUT. YOU CAN STOP ADVANCING IN LIFE & TRY TO JUST STAY IN THE SAME PLACE, BUT THE PERPETUAL ADVANCEMENT OF THE UNIVERSE WILL START THROWING MAJOR OBSTACLES & ENEMIES IN YOUR WAY TO GET YOU OUT OF THAT HOLDING PATTERN. THE UNIVERSE WOULD RATHER KILL YOU THAN HAVE YOU STALL OUT IF YOU'RE GOING TO WASTE YOUR LIFE. DON'T WASTE YOUR QUARTER.

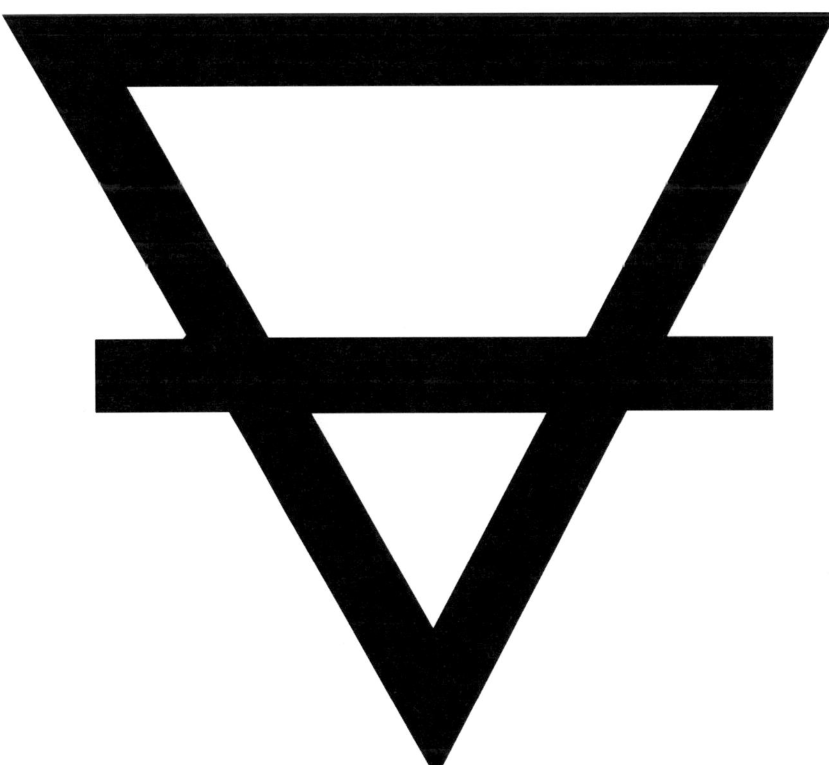

Life gives you plenty of opportunities to just live. It might seem that there is some kind of value to this, especially to us romantic types. When I was a teenager, just living was my biggest goal. I held it up as some kind of answer to the problems of society. But, I should point out that entire peoples get stuck on life & just do their thing while the rest of the world keeps spinning. There is definitely an advantage to progress & a problem with stagnation, if only because this sort of disintegration leads to non-existence which prevents the game from being played.

7. THE HUMAN MIND ONLY INTERPRETS WHAT IT PERCEIVES AS REALITY. WE DO NOT KNOW WHAT REALITY IS - BUT WE FEEL REALITY INTUITIVELY. ALL EXPRESSIONS OF REALITY ARE INTERPRETATIONS. FOLLOW YOUR NOSE.

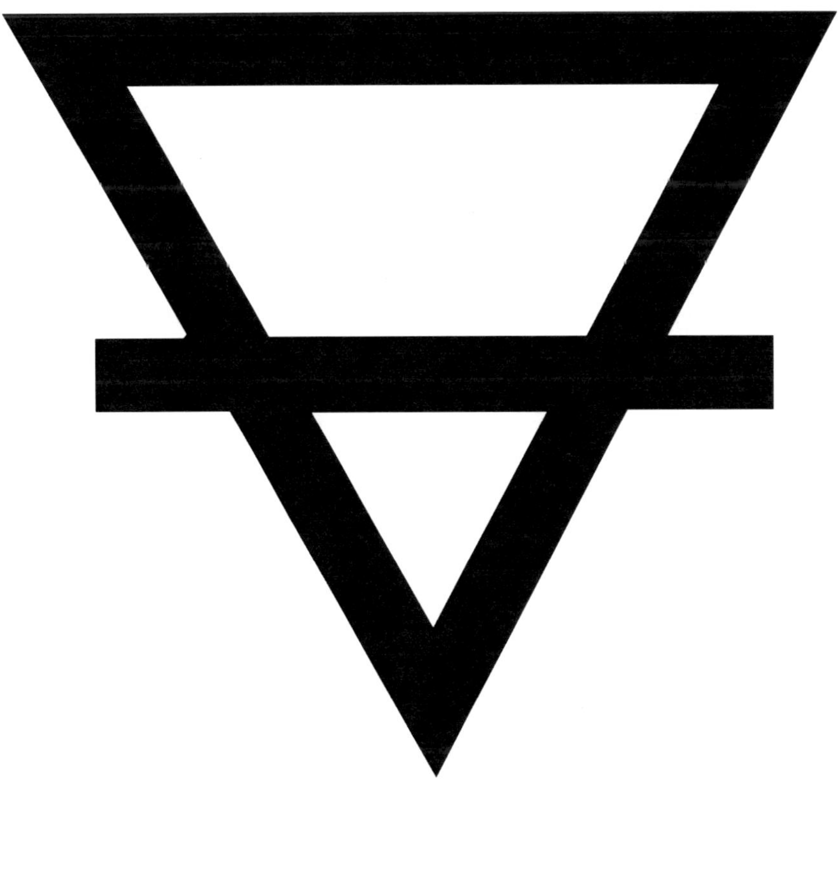

We only see, smell, touch, taste & hear certain things. The stroke knocked out my receptors for feeling temperature on my right side, but I know from experience that things are hot or cold. We have created machines that aid us in sensing the things around us that we can't perceive normally. I've seen & experienced that there is much more to reality than our five senses & it has been proven that there is more going on. One has only to look at the world of insects & pheromones to gain basic insight into this. I remember that depressive episodes in my head were set off by changes in atmospheric pressure. So, while going through a depressive spot felt just as bad as it always did, knowing a trigger & that it was temporary helped me gain perspective over it & helped me to see that there was a cause & that it would be temporary. So, while depression still felt as gloomy & hopeless as always, tainting my existence I knew that it would dissipate & I could go back to being my normal, cheery self.

Reality can be a divisive term for people because many use their view of reality as a means of control. This says more about the nature of humans & control than it does about the nature of reality. It is crucial to understand that reality is real & the same for everyone & that human perception of & description of reality is the relative thing. This is another reason why each game is totally individualized, it must be on account of the individual uniqueness, even if there are certain commonalities. Everyone is interfacing with the same reality though their perceptions widely differ. That is to say, the game is ultimately the same but each person is different.

Following your nose & developing your intuition enough to trust is difficult. Sometimes one's intuition is just wrong, no matter what you do. If you know that you have a lack of intuition on a certain thing, you must ask someone with the level

& specificity of intuition that you want what they think about the situation. There are plenty of things where I know my intuition is off, this is why it's so valuable to have a smart wife to bounce ideas off of & to find a complimentary partner in general.

8. PEOPLE WILL TRY TO TELL YOU WHAT THE GAME IS BUT THEY ARE ALWAYS WRONG. THEY WILL CREATE GAMES INSIDE OF THE GAME & TELL YOU THAT THEY HAVE THE GAME. THEY DON'T. THE GAME IS DIFFERENT FOR EVERY PLAYER. GAMES INSIDE OF THE GAME ARE JUST GAMES.

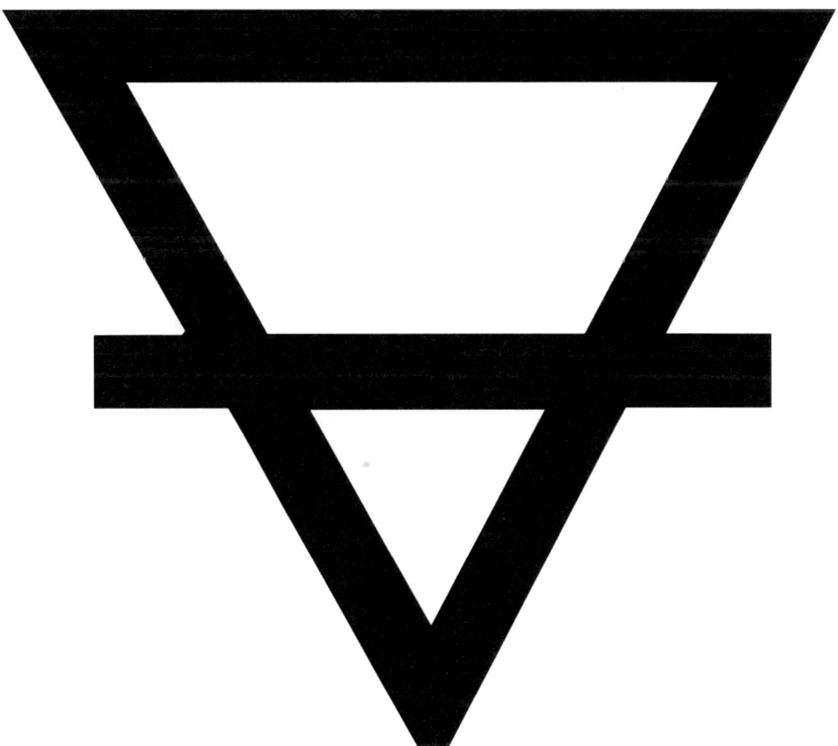

While pointing out that life is a game seems like it contradicts the point that I am telling you what the game is, the point is to let you know that life is a game. In pointing out that life is a game & how the game comes into each person as deeply individual, I am not making a new game for you, I am telling you about the nature of reality. One must understand the nature of reality to truly succeed in life.

There are plenty of games inside the Game that people have set up. These are just regular games & while some of them can make you or break you, they are not the infinitely individualized Game that everyone must figure out for themself. Sometimes these games are totally correct to play & hold great repositories of knowledge, great art, characters to unlock, missions to beat. But remember that they are not THE Game. Once you see these other games as methods of attempting to control reality it is almost impossible to go back to seeing them any other way. Most of the games are made to siphon money from people's pockets, but money is just a representation of power, stored energy & time.

Going to art school was one of the missions I had early on. I thought the goal would be to complete art school but completion was not the actual goal. Instead I met my wife, read a lot of art magazines, learned photoshop & dropped out, not having any desire to attend college ever again. I figured out that I didn't belong in art school quickly. I had too much direction for school, I wasn't a good student, I should have been teaching classes, not taking them. Although, I was too young & pointed to be a good teacher. There were a bunch of lessons I needed to learn first.

9. YOU ARE THE FINAL BOSS

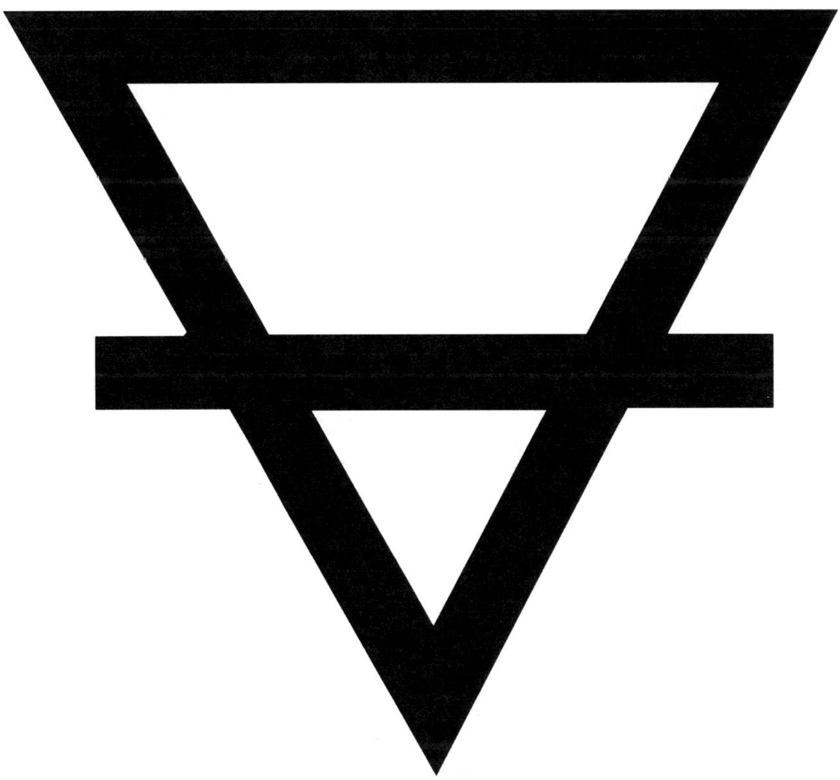

Eventually you wake up to the fact that you must face yourself & that all external opposition has been leading up to a point. Your "final judgment" is if you have been playing the Game according to the rules you've figured out thus far. Any guilt you have is from unfinished tasks that have accumulated along the way. You might be unlucky & have personalized the rule systems of others & have to confront those things when you die, but that's one of the best cases ever for not following other people's rules. I died when I had the stroke but they were able to resuscitate me. I didn't have any profound feelings of guilt or incompletion, although as I spent the next three months in the hospital, I was unsure of the future & the lack of an ability to plan & scheme accurately weighed on me terribly. But, I've always lived life by my own rules, so I was ready to die.

My observation of death is there is no afterlife. No Heaven, no Hell. The spirit is an energy that can be transferred, refined, captured etc. For the birth of each of our children I worked at transferring some of the spirit of people I admired into them. Flaky but true. Our ego wishes for there to be eternal life, an afterlife, important past lives, some kind of surety. This desire for surety is a product of the ego, but no such thing exists. But, it appears that the human soul leaves the body some time after death & then enters new lives in fragments, but I don't know this, this is just my observation. I'm not really interested in pursuing this notion or arguing one way or another. When I died, I experienced ego death. I am internally very different from who I was previously. I highly recommend ego death, it makes living a lot easier.

So, the Rules aren't so much rules, they're more about communicating an observation. I like rules, I also have no problem ignoring, breaking or making rules. This fluid attitude towards rules makes it very easy for me to look at a rule system & accept what is useful or true & discard what is a hindrance or false. It also makes me very difficult to understand for people that respect the rules. I am not bound by rules, & I don't think you should be either.

x SEAN
Summer 2023
Portland, OR